How To Reduce Stress and Improve Your Mental Health for Seniors

" A Comprehensive Guide for Seniors to Reduce Stress, Cultivate Resilience, and Transform Mental Well-Being"

Navil Gandhi

1

TABLE OF CONTENTS

INTRODUCTION

Navigating the Golden Years with Grace and Resilience**
The golden years are a chapter to be welcomed with wisdom, joy, and a dash of adventure in the tapestry of life. A new dawn, one that promises leisure, introspection, and the long-delayed pursuit of passions, emerges as the sun sets on the hectic days of our past. But among the benefits of becoming older, there's a silent partner that frequently goes hand in hand with seniors: the delicate balancing act between wellbeing and mental health.

Welcome to "How to Reduce Stress and Improve Your Mental Health for Seniors," a carefully thought-out manual for people enduring the rewarding but difficult process of aging. Using our thirty years of expertise as a reliable publisher, we set out on an engrossing investigation into the methods, ideas, and approaches that enable seniors to not just endure life's storms but to flourish in the midst of them.

"Unraveling the Mystery of Senior Mental Health".

We solve the puzzles of senior mental health in the first few chapters, offering a guide to the complexities of the aging mind. The aging brain, which is frequently undervalued and misinterpreted, becomes the main source of knowledge when we explore the typical difficulties that seniors encounter when pursuing mental wellness. We address the stigma associated with mental health among the elderly with empathy and clarity, laying the groundwork for a narrative that emphasizes mental health as a crucial aspect of aging gracefully.

Related to Stress and Mental Health

We examine the complex relationship between stress and mental health in Chapter 2. Stress is a commonplace companion in today's world, but if it isn't managed, it can cloud your golden years. We interpret the language of stress, pinpointing senior-specific triggers and shedding light on the compounding consequences of long-term stress. But do not be alarmed; acknowledging stress is not the end of our path. Rather, we set out on a comprehensive investigation of stress management techniques tailored to the special requirements of the elderly.

Whole-person Methods: Emotion, Body, and Spirit

In Chapter 3, a variety of holistic strategies for nourishing the body, mind, and spirit are woven together. This chapter provides guidance on promoting resilience and vitality, covering everything from the restorative effects of exercise to brain-boosting foods and the renewing benefits of relaxation practices. The significance of getting enough good sleep, which is sometimes overlooked, comes into focus as we realize how much it affects mental health.

Creatively Connecting and Strengthening Social Networks

We devote a whole chapter to the skill of creating and managing a helpful social network in the middle of our adventure. Seniors are invited to delve into the wide world of mental challenges, brain training, and creative endeavors that not only keep the mind active but also give life meaning and happiness.

Through the ensuing chapters, we will learn the importance of getting expert assistance, coping mechanisms for change and loss, and the transformational potential of fostering a healthy atmosphere. Often disregarded, financial wellbeing is essential to a safe and stress-free retirement.

We cordially invite you to join us on this insightful journey, which we hope will enable you or your loved ones to handle the golden years with grace, resiliency, and a fresh appreciation for the gifts that lie ahead in life's latter chapters. Let's set out on a journey together to celebrate the colorful tapestry that is aging and to experience less stress and better mental health. A life well lived is the goal, and the journey starts here.

CHAPTER 1

UNDERSTANDING SENIOR MENTAL HEALTH

The Aging Brain: What You Need to Know

Over the course of life, aging brings about a symphony of changes, and nowhere is this more apparent than in the intricate workings of the human brain. A vital investigation of the physiological changes that take place in the brain as we age gracefully, "The Aging Brain: What You Need to Know," is available. This chapter provides ideas that are both illuminating and empowering, acting as a cornerstone for comprehending the subtleties of senior mental health.

Understanding the immense intricacy and tenacity of this amazing organ is the first step towards embarking on a trip into the aging brain. The brain naturally ages over the years, changing both structurally and functionally. Although it is normal for cognitive capacities to change as we age, it is equally important to debunk myths and misconceptions that could raise doubts about the possibility of maintaining mental acuity.

The brain's capacity to rearrange itself by creating new synaptic connections throughout life is known as neuroplasticity, and it is a crucial feature of the aging process. Research has shown that the brain is flexible and receptive to new experiences, learning, and environmental stimuli well into old age, defying previous assumptions. This insight dispels the myth that cognitive decline is a natural byproduct of aging, serving as a ray of hope.

The chapter does, however, also openly discuss the changes that actually take place. Changes in neurotransmitter levels and brain mass may be examples of structural modifications that lead to changes in cognitive performance. Rather than focusing on restrictions, it is important to recognize these shifts and provide people with the knowledge they need to negotiate this new terrain with resilience and proactivity.

Most importantly, this chapter emphasizes how critical it is to continue treating brain health from a holistic perspective. It explores the mutually reinforcing nature of physical and mental health, highlighting the influence of lifestyle choices like nutrition, exercise, and sleep on mental capacity. Seniors may actively help to preserve and improve their cognitive capacities by taking a proactive approach to brain health.

The chapter also discusses typical issues, including forgetfulness and cognitive decline, highlighting the distinctions between age-related changes that are expected and possible indicators of more serious illnesses. In addition to reducing needless anxiety, this demystification promotes early intervention when needed.

Common Mental Health Challenges for Seniors

Seniors, like individuals in any other age group, may face various mental health challenges. However, aging can bring unique factors that contribute to specific mental health concerns. Here are some common mental health challenges that seniors may encounter:

1. Depression: Depression is a prevalent mental health issue among seniors. Factors such as chronic health conditions, social isolation, the loss of loved ones, and changes in life circumstances can contribute to feelings of sadness, hopelessness, and despair.

2. Anxiety Disorders: Seniors may experience anxiety related to health concerns, financial worries, or the fear of losing independence. Generalized anxiety disorder, phobias, and panic disorder are examples of anxiety disorders that can affect older individuals.

3. Cognitive Decline and Dementia: Cognitive decline, including conditions like Alzheimer's disease and other forms of dementia, is a significant mental health challenge for seniors. Memory loss, confusion, and changes in cognitive abilities can have a profound impact on an individual's mental well-being.

4. Grief and Loss: Seniors often face multiple losses, including the deaths of friends, spouses, or family members. Grieving these losses is a natural part of life, but prolonged grief or complicated bereavement can lead to mental health challenges.

5. Isolation and Loneliness: Social isolation is a common issue among seniors, especially those who may be living alone or in long-term care facilities. Lack of social interaction can contribute to feelings of loneliness, which, in turn, can negatively impact mental health.

6. Chronic Health Conditions: Managing chronic health conditions, such as diabetes, arthritis, or cardiovascular diseases, can be mentally taxing. The burden of coping with ongoing health challenges may contribute to stress, anxiety, or depression.

7. Sleep Disorders: Older adults often experience changes in sleep patterns, including difficulty falling asleep or staying asleep. Sleep disturbances can exacerbate mental health issues and contribute to feelings of fatigue and irritability.

8. Substance Abuse: Some seniors may turn to alcohol or prescription medications as a way to cope with stress, pain, or mental health issues. Substance abuse can complicate existing mental health challenges and contribute to further physical health problems.

9. Adjustment Disorders: Life transitions, such as retirement, relocation, or changes in health status, can trigger adjustment disorders. Difficulty adapting to new circumstances may lead to symptoms like anxiety or depression.

10. Financial Stress: Financial concerns, including worries about retirement savings, healthcare costs, or economic instability, can contribute to mental health challenges in seniors.

Breaking the Stigma: Addressing Mental Health in the Elderly

Breaking the Stigma: Addressing Mental Health in the Elderly

There is a pressing need to shed light on the murky areas of mental health in the complex tapestry of aging, where the colors of experience increase and the threads of knowledge are sewn. "Breaking the Stigma: Addressing Mental Health in the Elderly" becomes a call to action, a crucial conversation that cuts across generations and demolishes the myths surrounding seniors' mental health.

The Hidden Challenges Faced by the Elderly

The attitudes and conventions of society have, for far too long, encouraged a culture of silence regarding the mental health of the elderly. Seniors who struggle with mental health concerns may experience underreporting, incorrect diagnoses, and inadequate care due to the stigma attached to these conditions. This chapter aims to shed light on the hidden battles and promote empathy for the emotional terrain that goes along with the aging process. Unnecessary anxiety but also to encourage early intervention when necessary.

Challenging Preconceptions

Dispelling long-held misconceptions and expectations about mental health is essential to the effort to end the stigma. With aging, mental health changes in the same ways as physical health does. This chapter aims to dispel myths that could support the idea that mental health issues are an inevitable part of growing older. Seniors are not immune to the complexity of the mind.

The Influence of Knowledge and Awareness

The foundation of this campaign is education. By raising awareness of the range and frequency of mental health issues that affect the elderly, we enable people—individuals, families, and communities—to spot the warning signs and get the help they need. Change is sparked by awareness, which makes it possible to move from isolation to empathy and from judgment to communal support.

A Request for Action

"Breaking the Stigma" is a call to action as much as an investigation. It exhorts readers to have candid discussions on mental health in order to create a space where elderly people may open up about their experiences without worrying about being judged. In order to ensure that resources and support systems are easily accessible, this chapter calls on healthcare professionals, caregivers, and community leaders to support policies that prioritize mental health in elder care.

Narratives of Resilience

This chapter is filled with success stories and tales of resiliency from seniors who have persevered through severe mental health difficulties. These testimonies honor the tenacious nature of these individuals. These tales act as rays of hope, showing that mental health treatment is not only feasible but also a lifelong process with the correct assistance.

CHAPTER 2

THE CONNECTION BETWEEN STRESS AND MENTAL HEALTH

Defining Stress and Its Impact on Mental Well-being

Stress is a common song in the big symphony of life, affecting everyone of us differently and to varying degrees. Understanding the subtleties of this ubiquitous force that can influence the story of our mental health is essential to navigating the complex tango between stress and mental health.

Defining Stress: Beyond Daily Pressures" Stress is essentially the body's reaction to a perceived threat or challenge. Although stressful events are frequently linked to bad experiences, it's important to understand that not all stress is bad. Eustress, or positive stress, can invigorate and inspire people, helping them to reach their objectives. But stress can become a major issue impacting mental health when it becomes persistent or overpowering.

The first step in this chapter is to examine the various facets of stress. The complex interactions between hormones like cortisol and the physiological reactions set off by the sympathetic nervous system provide readers with insights into the complex mechanisms underlying the stress response. It is more than just a mental condition; it is an intricate coordination of the body and mind.

Recognizing Stress Triggers in Seniors

Recognizing the particular difficulties elders may encounter is necessary to comprehend stress in this context. Stressors for the elderly population might include everything from health issues and money problems to bereavement and retirement-related adjustments. Determining these stressors is critical to developing specialized solutions that lessen their negative effects on mental health.

The Cumulative Effect: Chronic Stress and Its Consequences

As we go further, the chapter delves into the idea of chronic stress, which is a persistent condition that, over time, can have a negative impact on mental health. Anxiety, despair, and cognitive impairment are just a few of the mental health issues that can arise after a lifetime of pressure. Because age-related factors may aggravate the effects of chronic stress, seniors in particular may be particularly vulnerable to it.

Analyzing the effects of long-term stress on mental health reveals a terrain characterized by disturbed sleep, emotional swings, and impaired cognitive abilities. Chronic stress has also been connected to a higher chance of acquiring or aggravating a number of physical health issues, highlighting the complex relationship between mental and physical health.

Recognizing Stress Triggers in Seniors

Recognizing stress triggers in seniors requires a combination of observation, open communication, and a nuanced understanding of the unique challenges they may face. Here are some practical strategies to help identify stress triggers in seniors:

1.Open Communication:

- Encourage open and honest communication. Create a safe space where seniors feel comfortable expressing their thoughts and feelings without fear of judgment.
- Initiate conversations about their daily experiences, concerns, and any recent changes in their lives. Actively listen to their responses, paying attention to both verbal and non-verbal cues.

3. Observe Behavioral Changes:

- Be attentive to changes in behavior. Increased irritability, mood swings, withdrawal from social activities, or alterations in sleep patterns can indicate heightened stress levels.
- Notice any changes in appetite, energy levels, or the ability to concentrate. These behavioral changes can be indicators of underlying stressors.

4. Life Transitions:

Recognize that life transitions, such as retirement, loss of a spouse, moving to a new living arrangement, or coping with chronic illness, can be significant stressors. These changes may require adjustments that can affect mental well-being.

5. Financial Concerns:

- Seniors may worry about financial stability, especially if they are on a fixed income. Discuss financial matters sensitively, addressing any concerns or uncertainties they may have about their financial situation.

6. Loss and Grief:

- Loss of friends, family members, or close peers can be a profound stress trigger. Grieving is a natural process, but prolonged or complicated grief may contribute to mental health challenges.

7. Social Isolation:

- Social isolation is a common stressor for seniors. Pay attention to their social interactions and support systems. Loneliness can have a significant impact on mental well-being.

8. Cognitive Changes:

- Cognitive decline or the fear of it can be a stress trigger. Recognize any signs of memory loss, confusion, or difficulty in decision-making. Addressing these concerns early can alleviate stress.

9. Environmental Factors:

- Evaluate the living environment. Issues like inadequate housing, safety concerns, or a lack of accessibility can contribute to stress. Ensure that the senior's living conditions support their well-being.

10. Changes in Routine:

- Seniors often find comfort in routine. Disruptions to established routines, whether due to external factors or health changes, can be stressors. Monitor any adjustments in their daily activities.

11. Technology Challenges:

Technological advancements can sometimes be stressful for seniors. If they face difficulties with new devices or feel left behind in the digital age, it can lead to frustration and stress.

Remember that recognizing stress triggers is an ongoing process, and it requires sensitivity and patience. By fostering open communication and actively addressing the concerns identified, you can play a crucial role in supporting the mental well-being of the seniors in your care.

The Cumulative Effect: Chronic Stress and Its Consequences

The cumulative effect of chronic stress on an The impact on a person's physical and mental health can be significant and far-reaching. When the body's stress response is triggered over an extended period of time, stress hormones like cortisol are continuously released, which is known as chronic stress. The effects of ongoing stress can take several forms in the case of seniors, impacting their mental and physical well-being. The following are some salient features of the compounding consequences of long-term stress:

1. Cognitive Impairment:

Prolonged stress has been linked to memory loss and a higher chance of neurodegenerative diseases like Alzheimer's. Long-term exposure to stress hormones may impede memory and other cognitive processes as well as cause anatomical alterations in the brain. both physical and mental well-being. The following are some salient features of the compounding consequences of long-term stress:

2. Emotional Well-being:

Prolonged stress can negatively impact mental health and raise the risk of anxiety and depression. Seniors who are under chronic stress may display signs including increased anxiety, despondency, or a lingering sense of sadness.

3. Cardiovascular Health:

Persistent stress raises the risk of heart disease and causes hypertension, or high blood pressure, among other cardiovascular problems. Increased stress hormones have the potential to cause cardiovascular issues by influencing blood vessel function and inflaming the body.

4. Weakened Immune System:

Prolonged stress may impair the immune system's capacity to fight off infections. Prolonged stress in seniors may make them more susceptible to disease and extend the time it takes them to recover from infections.

5. Digestive Problems:

Chronic stress can disrupt the digestive system, leading to issues such as indigestion, irritable bowel syndrome (IBS), or exacerbating - Prolonged stress can cause digestive system disruptions, which can aggravate pre-existing gastrointestinal disorders or cause problems like indigestion and irritable bowel syndrome (IBS). Nutritional difficulties may also be caused by changes in appetite and eating habits brought on by stress.

6. Sleep Disturbances:

Seniors who are under a lot of stress on a regular basis may have trouble sleeping, which includes trouble getting to sleep, staying asleep, or getting restorative sleep. Difficulties with mental and physical health are further exacerbated by little or poor-quality sleep.

7. Pain Perception:

Persistent stress has the ability to intensify pain perception. Seniors with chronic pain disorders may be more sensitive to discomfort, which makes managing their pain more difficult.

8. Endocrine Disruption:

Prolonged stress can cause disruptions to the endocrine system, which controls hormones. This could lead to hormone imbalances, which could affect many body functions and perhaps exacerbate diseases like diabetes.

9. Accelerated Aging:

According to certain research, long-term stress may hasten cellular aging. Protective caps on the ends of chromosomes called telomeres may shorten more quickly in people who are under constant stress, which may have an effect on longevity and general health.

10. Impact on Mental Health Services:

Persistent stress can make it more difficult to treat pre-existing mental health issues. Chronic stress can make symptoms worse for seniors who suffer from disorders like depression or anxiety and reduce the efficacy of treatment.

CHAPTER 3

HOLISTIC APPROACHES TO STRESS REDUCTION

Mind-Body Connection: The Power of Relaxation Techniques

The body and mind are closely related, constantly affecting one another in a dance that determines our general state of well-being. Promoting mental health can be effectively achieved by comprehending and utilizing the mind-body connection, particularly in the setting of senior citizens. This chapter reveals the transforming power of practices that promote harmony between these two fundamental parts of the human experience by examining the significant effects of relaxation techniques on the mind and body.

The Interwoven Web of Mind and Body: According to the theory of the mind-body link, our emotional and mental states have a significant impact on our physical health, and vice versa. Seniors are especially sensitive to this complex interaction since they may have lived a lifetime filled with both pleasures and difficulties. Age-related stressors and life experiences' cumulative effects call for a holistic strategy that recognizes the mutually reinforcing nature of mental and physical health.

Understanding the Stress Response:

Stress, a constant companion in life, sets off the body's "fight or flight" reaction. While an invaluable ancestral survival mechanism in the face of acute threats, persistent activation of this mechanism can have deleterious effects. Stress hormones that are elevated, such as cortisol, can affect the immunological system, the cardiovascular system, and even age-related cognitive decline. Techniques that control this stress response can be quite beneficial for seniors, who frequently face specific pressures.

The Power of Relaxation Techniques:

Let me introduce you to relaxation techniques, a collection of exercises that lead the body and mind into a peaceful dance. A range of approaches, such as progressive muscle relaxation, guided imagery, and mindfulness meditation, can help elders manage the intricacies of stress and cultivate a sense of calm.

1. Deep Breathing Exercises:

Deep, controlled breathing causes the body to go into relaxation mode, drop blood pressure, and slow its heart rate. Simple breathing techniques can help seniors feel less stressed and have better mental clarity.

2. Progressive Muscle Relaxation:

This method entails methodically tensing and relaxing various muscle groups. It increases awareness of physical sensations and encourages physical relaxation, creating a mind-body connection that releases stress.

3. Guided Imagery:

Seniors engaged in visualization exercises are transported to serene, imagined settings. Through guided imagery that stimulates the senses, people can construct mental environments that support emotional stability and relaxation.

4. Mindfulness Meditation:

Mindfulness promotes judgment-free present-moment awareness. Seniors can develop resilience and lessen the effects of stress by learning to monitor their thoughts and feelings without being overwhelmed.

5. Yoga and Tai Chi:

Integrative exercises that combine breath awareness and gentle movement are yoga and tai chi. These senior-friendly hobbies provide mental and physical relaxation as well as balance and flexibility.

Benefits for Seniors

There are several advantages to using relaxation techniques with senior citizens. From a physical standpoint, these exercises help lower stress hormones, promote better sleep, and strengthen the immune system. In terms of mental health, they foster emotional resilience, lessen depressive and anxious symptoms, and offer strategies for handling the stresses that come with growing older.

Empowering Seniors to Thrive:

This chapter serves as both guidance and an invitation for seniors to set out on a path of self-awareness and empowerment. Seniors can develop a sense of well-being that outlives the difficulties of aging by accepting the mind-body connection and implementing relaxation practices into their daily lives. One breath and one relaxation technique at a time, the possibility for a lively and meaningful senior life arises when the mind and body synchronize.

The Role of Exercise in Alleviating Stress

Exercise has many advantages that go well beyond improving physical health and make it a potent remedy for life's stresses. This chapter delves into the complex relationship between physical activity and stress alleviation, revealing the extraordinary ways in which exercise acts as a natural and approachable solution for the mental and emotional problems that older adults confront.

Stress and the Body: Understanding the Dynamics:

Prior to discussing the function of exercise, it is important to comprehend how stress affects the body. Chronic stress causes the body to release stress chemicals like cortisol, which can have detrimental effects on both physical and mental health. The body's "fight or flight" reaction can become maladaptive if it is triggered frequently, even while it is adaptive in the short term.

Exercise as a Natural Stress Reliever:

Let's talk about exercise, a powerful weapon in the fight against stress. Regular physical activity offers several advantages, one of which is its significant reduction of stress. Here's how exercise reduces stress naturally:

1. Release of Endorphins:

Endorphins, the body's natural mood enhancers, are released when exercise is performed. These neurochemicals produce a feeling of bliss and well-being by acting as organic stress and pain relievers.

2. Reduction of Stress Hormones:

Exercise aids in the control of stress chemicals like cortisol. Frequent exercise reduces the long-term rise in cortisol levels, averting the negative consequences of ongoing stress.

3. Improved Sleep Quality:

Regular exercise has been associated with better sleep. Recovering from stress requires good sleep, and sleep's restorative qualities support mental toughness in general.

4. Distraction and Relaxation:

Exercising offers a constructive diversion from pressures. Exercise, whether it be a yoga class, a brisk walk, or a swim, provides a break, enabling people to change their focus and clear their minds.

5. Enhanced Mood and Emotional Resilience:
Exercise has been linked to increased emotional fortitude and mood. It promotes optimism and a sense of control while assisting people in managing life's obstacles.

6. Social engagement:

Engaging in physical activities or group exercise might offer chances for social engagement. Social support, which provides a feeling of community and connection, is essential for stress management.

Senior Tailoring Exercise:

Including exercise in daily life can have a profoundly positive impact on seniors. It's important to customize workout plans for each person, taking into account things like mobility, degree of fitness, and any pre-existing medical issues. Seniors should take into account the following:

1. Low-Impact Activities:

Exercises that are easy on the joints but yet beneficial to the heart include walking, swimming, and cycling. Exercises with low impact lower the chance of injury and are well suited for seniors.

2. Strength Training:

For seniors, developing and preserving physical strength is crucial. Exercises for strength training that use resistance bands, small weights, or your own body weight can enhance joint health and general strength.

3. Flexibility and Balance:

Seniors might benefit from exercises like yoga or tai chi that improve flexibility and balance. These exercises not only enhance physical performance but also encourage unwinding and lower stress levels.

4. Sustained, Regular Routine:

Maintaining consistency is essential. Seniors ought to strive for a consistent and long-lasting fitness regimen. Throughout the day, even little periods of activity can improve general wellbeing.

Nutrition for Brain Health: Foods that Nourish the Mind

The connection between nutrition and brain health is a topic of growing importance, especially as individuals age and seek to optimize cognitive function. This chapter explores the vital role of nutrition in supporting brain health, unveiling a palette of foods that not only nourish the body but also fuel the mind for optimal mental well-being, especially in the senior years.

The Brain's Appetite for Nutrients:

The brain, a marvel of complexity, demands a steady supply of nutrients to function at its best. From energy production and neurotransmitter synthesis to protection against oxidative stress, the right balance of nutrients plays a crucial role in maintaining cognitive health.

Omega-3 Fatty Acids:

Sources:

Fatty fish (such as salmon, trout, and sardines), flaxseeds

 chia seeds

 and walnuts.

Benefits:

 Omega-3 fatty acids, particularly EPA and DHA, are essential for brain structure and function. They support neuronal membranes, promote synaptic plasticity, and have anti-inflammatory effects that may protect the brain.

Antioxidant-rich Fruits and Vegetables:

Sources:

Berries (blueberries, strawberries, and raspberries), dark leafy greens, broccoli, tomatoes, and oranges.

- **Benefits:**

Antioxidants, such as vitamins C and E, help combat oxidative stress in the brain. These compounds neutralize free radicals, reducing the risk of cellular damage and inflammation.

Whole Grains:

Sources: Quinoa, brown rice, whole wheat, and oats.

- Benefits: Whole grains provide a steady supply of glucose, the brain's primary energy source. They also contain fiber, which supports healthy digestion and helps regulate blood sugar levels.

Nuts and Seeds:

Sources: Almonds, walnuts, sunflower seeds, pumpkin seeds.

- Benefits: Rich in vitamin E, antioxidants, and healthy fats, nuts and seeds contribute to cognitive health. Vitamin E, in particular, has been associated with a lower risk of cognitive decline in aging.

Dark Chocolate:

Sources: Dark chocolate with a high cocoa content (70% or more).

- **Benefits:** Dark chocolate contains flavonoids, caffeine, and antioxidants that may improve memory and cognitive function. Moderation is key due to its calorie density.

Fruits with High Antioxidant Content:

Sources: Avocado, pomegranate, and acerola cherries.

- **Benefits:** These fruits are rich in antioxidants, healthy fats, and vitamins that contribute to overall brain health and may support cognitive function.

Fatty Fish:

Sources: Salmon, trout, mackerel, herring.

- **Benefits:** Fatty fish are abundant in omega-3 fatty acids, which are crucial for brain health. Regular consumption is associated with a lower risk of cognitive decline and improved mental well-being.

Turmeric:

Sources: Turmeric spice (contains curcumin).

- **Benefits:** Curcumin, the active compound in turmeric, has anti-inflammatory and antioxidant properties. Some studies suggest it may have neuroprotective effects and contribute to brain health.

Legumes:

Sources: lentils, chickpeas, and black beans.

- **Benefits:** Legumes are rich in complex carbohydrates, fiber, and protein. They provide a steady release of energy and contribute to overall brain function.

Green Tea:

Sources: Green tea leaves.

- **Benefits:** Green tea contains caffeine and L-theanine, which can enhance cognitive performance and promote alertness without the jittery effects associated with excessive caffeine consumption.

The Importance of Hydration:

Sources: Water, herbal teas.

- **Benefits:** Staying well-hydrated is essential for cognitive function. Dehydration can impair concentration and memory, so maintaining adequate fluid intake is a simple yet vital aspect of brain health.

Importance of Adequate Sleep for Senior Mental Wellness

 Adequate sleep is of paramount importance for senior mental wellness, playing a crucial role in maintaining cognitive function, emotional well-being, and overall quality of life. As individuals age, sleep patterns may change, and seniors often face specific challenges that can impact the duration and quality of their sleep. Understanding the importance of sufficient and restorative sleep for seniors is vital for promoting mental health and overall well-being. Here are key aspects highlighting the significance of adequate sleep for senior mental wellness:

1. Cognitive Function:

Memory and Learning: Quality sleep is essential for memory consolidation and learning. Seniors who get sufficient sleep are better able to retain and recall information, supporting cognitive functions crucial for daily activities and problem-solving.

2. Emotional Regulation:

Mood Stability: Sleep influences emotional regulation, and inadequate sleep can contribute to irritability, mood swings, and increased vulnerability to stress. Seniors who prioritize good sleep hygiene are better equipped to manage their emotions and maintain a positive outlook.

3. Attention and Concentration:

Sustained Attention: Adequate sleep supports sustained attention and concentration. Seniors who prioritize sleep are more likely to stay focused on tasks, make informed decisions, and engage in activities that contribute to mental stimulation.

4. Stress Resilience:

Stress Reduction: Quality sleep plays a crucial role in stress resilience. Seniors who get enough restorative sleep are better equipped to cope with life's challenges, and their ability to manage stress is enhanced.

5. Prevention of Cognitive Decline:

Reduced Risk of Cognitive Disorders: Chronic sleep deprivation has been linked to an increased risk of cognitive disorders such as Alzheimer's disease and dementia. Prioritizing adequate sleep may contribute to the prevention of cognitive decline.

6. Improved Mental Health:

Reduced Risk of Depression: Insufficient sleep is associated with an increased risk of depression in seniors. Prioritizing sleep hygiene and addressing sleep-related issues can contribute to improved mental health outcomes.

7. Enhanced Immune Function:

Immune Support: Quality sleep is essential for maintaining a robust immune system. Seniors with adequate sleep are better equipped to resist infections and promote overall physical health, indirectly supporting mental well-being.

8. Management of Chronic Conditions:

Impact on Chronic Health Conditions: Seniors often manage chronic health conditions, and adequate sleep is a key factor in their overall health management. Quality sleep can positively influence conditions such as diabetes, cardiovascular issues, and pain management.

9. Safety and Independence:

Reduced Fall Risk: Poor sleep quality can contribute to an increased risk of falls, especially among seniors. Prioritizing good sleep hygiene promotes safety, independence, and an overall higher quality of life.

10. Enhanced Quality of Life:

Overall Well-Being: Quality sleep is foundational to an individual's overall well-being. Seniors who consistently enjoy adequate, restorative sleep are more likely to experience an enhanced quality of life, both mentally and physically.

Promoting Good Sleep Hygiene in Seniors:

Encouraging good sleep hygiene practices is crucial for seniors to reap the benefits of adequate sleep. This may include:

- establishing a regular sleep schedule.
- creating a comfortable sleep environment.
- Limiting stimulants like caffeine and electronics before bedtime.
- engaging in relaxing activities before sleep.

CHAPTER 4

BUILDING A SUPPORTIVE SOCIAL NETWORK

The Impact of Social Isolation on Senior Mental Health

Seniors' mental health and general well-being can be significantly impacted by social isolation, which is described as a lack of meaningful social contacts and relationships. Because they may have additional difficulties that exacerbate social isolation, elderly people are more likely to experience this phenomenon. Addressing the mental health needs of elders requires an understanding of the effects of social isolation. Key points emphasizing the negative effects of social isolation on senior mental health are as follows:

1. Depression Risk Increased:

- **Sadness and Loneliness:** Seniors who experience social isolation have a higher risk of depression. Depressive symptoms can arise or worsen as a result of experiencing feelings of abandonment, melancholy, and loneliness, all of which can have a negative impact on mental health.

2. Cognitive Decline:

- **Affect on Mental Process:** Social isolation has been linked to memory loss and a higher chance of acquiring dementia and Alzheimer's disease. Over time, cognitive capacities may deteriorate as a result of a lack of social contact.

3.Increased Stress Levels:

- **Heightened Anxiety and Stress:** Seniors who are socially isolated may feel more stressed and anxious. Lack of social support might make one feel more vulnerable and less able to handle stressful situations.

4. Difficult Effect on Physical Health:

- **Inhibited Immune Response:** Physical health might suffer from social isolation, which can weaken the immune system. Seniors without social networks could be more susceptible to disease and might take longer to recover.

5. Reduced Quality of Life:

- **Effect on General Well-Being:** Seniors who are socially isolated have a lower overall quality of life. Lack of social contacts can cause people to feel empty inside, be less satisfied with their lives, and believe that their quality of life is inferior.

6. Risk of Mortality Increased:

- **Correlates with Mortality:** Seniors who experience social isolation may have a higher chance of dying. An increased risk of early mortality can result from a loss of physical health brought on by a lack of social relationships.

7. Affect on Sleeping Patterns:

- **Disturbances in Sleep:** Seniors who are socially isolated may have trouble sleeping. Difficulties falling and keeping asleep can be attributed to feelings of loneliness and a lack of social involvement.

8. Limited Emotional Support:

- **Lack of Emotional Assistance:** Lack of emotional support, which is essential for mental health, results from social isolation. Socially isolated people frequently struggle with feeling understood, encouraged to share their experiences, and able to obtain support.

9. Lack of Mental Stimulation:

- **Reduced Cognitive Stimulation:** Cognitive stimulation is facilitated by social connections, while mental stagnation may result from their absence. Social interaction improves memory, problem-solving skills, and cognitive flexibility.

10. A Effect on Self-Esteem:

- **Reduced Self-Value:** Low self-esteem and a feeling of social rejection can be caused by social isolation. Seniors who don't regularly engage in social activities might start to doubt their worth and importance to society.

Addressing Social Isolation:

Understanding how social isolation affects senior mental health emphasizes how critical it is to implement solutions to deal with this problem.

Among the tactics might be:

- organizing social gatherings and activities.
- Promoting involvement in neighbourhood associations.
- encouraging volunteer work.
- using technology to establish virtual relationships.
- Promoting communication across generations.
- assisting older citizens with transportation so they can go to social activities.

Strategies for Building and Maintaining Social Connections

For general well-being, establishing and sustaining social ties is crucial, particularly for seniors who may be in danger of social isolation. The following techniques can assist seniors in creating and maintaining deep social relationships:

1. Involvement in the Community:

- **Join Groups and Clubs:** Seniors should be encouraged to join local clubs or interest groups. Joining a reading club, gardening club, or hobby club offers chances to connect with people who share your interests.

2. Volunteering:

- **Participate in Volunteer Work:** A rewarding way to give back to the community and make new friends is through volunteering. Seniors can look into opportunities with neighborhood organizations, schools, or charities.

3. Senior Centers and Community Centers:

- **Take Part in Senior Initiatives:** Senior-focused programs are available in many towns at community centers or senior centers. These programs frequently include social gatherings, workshops, and exercise classes.

4. Social media and Technology:

- **Utilize Technology for Communication:** Seniors can maintain relationships with friends and family by using social media and cellphones, among other forms of technology. Regular communication is made possible by social networking sites, messaging apps, and video calls.

5. Engage in Local Events:

- **Discover Local Events:** Seniors should be encouraged to participate in neighborhood festivals, celebrations, and get-togethers. These events offer chances to socialize and partake in activities with new people.

6. Activities for Intergenerations:

- **Take Part in Programs for Intergenerations:** It can be beneficial to interact with younger generations. Seniors can build relationships with younger people by taking part in intergenerational initiatives like mentoring or volunteering in schools.

7. Attend religious or spiritual services:

- **Take Part in Religious Communities:** If appropriate, seniors who attend religious or spiritual services and engage in related activities may feel a sense of belonging and community.

8. Remain Engaged:

- **Engage in Physical Exercise:** Frequent exercise facilitates social contact in addition to improving physical health. Elderly people can participate in walking clubs, fitness courses, and other physical activities.

9. Participate in Educational Workshops or Classes: Numerous communities provide workshops or classes on a range of topics. Seniors who want to meet new people and pick up new skills can do so by attending these educational sessions.

10. Friends and Family: Put family relationships first. Encourage family members to communicate on a regular basis. Family get-togethers and activities can offer a solid basis for social relationships.

11. Ownership of a Pet:

- **Think About Pet Companionship:** Pets can make excellent friends and offer chances for social connection. Making new friends with other pet owners can result from walking your dog or going to pet-related events.

12.Community Links:

- **Acquaint yourself with your neighbors.** Developing ties with neighbors helps to promote a sense of community. Seniors can plan social events, take part in neighborhood activities, and become members of neighborhood watch organizations.

CHAPTER 5

COGNITIVE EXERCISES AND BRAIN TRAINING

Keeping the Mind Sharp: Mental Exercises for Seniors

Maintaining mental acuity is essential for overall cognitive health, particularly as people get older. Regular mental exercise can help seniors maintain their mental health, improve their memory, and maintain their cognitive function. To help elders maintain mental acuity, consider the following variety of mental exercises:

1. Puzzles and Brain Games:

- **Crossword Puzzles:** These word puzzles challenge vocabulary and problem-solving skills.
- **Sudoku:** A number puzzle that exercises logical thinking and pattern recognition.
- **Jigsaw Puzzles:** Assembling pieces stimulates visual and spatial awareness and attention to detail.
- **Brain Training Apps:** Use apps like Lumosity or Elevate that offer a variety of brain games targeting memory, attention, and problem-solving.

2. Memory Exercises:

- **Memory Games:** Play games that involve remembering sequences, patterns, or lists of items.
- **Flashcards:** Create flashcards with information to memorize, such as historical facts, vocabulary, or names.
- **Recall Stories:** Practice recalling and retelling stories or events from memory.

3. Learn Something New:

- **Take Classes:** Enroll in classes or workshops to learn a new skill or hobby.
- **Language Learning:** Learning a new language stimulates the brain and enhances cognitive flexibility.
- **Musical Instruments:** Playing an instrument challenges memory, coordination, and auditory skills.

4. Reading and Discussion:

- **Book Clubs:** Join or form a book club to engage in reading and thoughtful discussions.

- **Current Affairs:** Stay informed about current events and engage in discussions to stimulate critical thinking.
- **Educational Articles:** Read articles on a variety of subjects to broaden your knowledge and perspectives.

5. Mindful Meditation:

- **Mindfulness Practices:** Engage in mindfulness meditation to enhance focus and reduce stress.
- **Deep Breathing:** Practice deep breathing exercises to promote relaxation and mental clarity.

6. Strategic Games:

- **Chess or Checkers:** Play strategic board games that require planning and critical thinking.
- **Card Games:** Games like bridge, poker, or solitaire stimulate memory and strategic thinking.
- **Strategy Video Games:** Some video games can provide mental stimulation and strategic challenges.

7. Cognitive Training Apps:

- **Word Games:** Apps like Words with Friends or Scrabble challenge vocabulary and strategic thinking.
- **Logic Puzzles:** Apps with logic puzzles or brainteasers provide mental challenges.
- **Memory Apps:** Specifically designed apps to improve memory and cognitive function.

8. Creative Writing:

- **Journaling:** Write about personal experiences, thoughts, or creative stories.
- **Poetry or Short Stories:** Engage in creative writing to foster imagination and linguistic abilities.
- **Memory Recall Writing:** Document personal memories and stories to exercise recall.

9. Visualization Exercises:

- **Mind's Eye Exercises:** Close your eyes and visualize scenes, objects, or detailed scenarios.
- **Memory Palaces:** Create mental images of places and use them to organize and remember information.

10. Social Interaction:

- **Conversation:** Engage in conversations with friends, family, or peers to stimulate cognitive functions.

- **Social Games:** Play games that involve interaction, such as charades or trivia with others.

11. Daily Mental Challenges:

- **Math Exercises:** Practice simple mental math or solve math problems to keep the brain active.

- **Riddles and Brainteasers:** Solve riddles or brainteasers to enhance problem-solving skills.

The Benefits of Hobbies and Creative Pursuits

Taking up artistic and recreational activities has many advantages for people of all ages. These pursuits improve one's physical, mental, and emotional health in addition to being enjoyable. The following are some of the main advantages of engaging in creative pursuits and hobbies:

1. Mental Stimulation:

- **Cognitive Functions:** The brain is stimulated by hobbies that require problem-solving, critical thinking, and learning new abilities; these activities may even be able to prevent cognitive decline.

2. Emotional Well-Being:

- **tension Reduction:** Taking part in pleasant activities can provide a quiet and relaxed atmosphere by relieving tension.

- **Mood Enhancement:** Engaging in creative endeavors can lead to feelings of joy and fulfillment, which can enhance mood and emotional health.

3. Social Interaction:

- **Building Community:** Hobbies offer chances to interact with people who share similar interests, which promotes a sense of community and lessens feelings of social isolation.

- **Friendship and camaraderie:** Hobbies in common can foster the development of social ties and friendships, which improves general social well-being.

4. Physical Health: Engaging in physical activities such as athletics, dancing, or gardening can enhance one's physical well-being and fitness.

Eye-Hand Coordination: Hands-on creative endeavors like painting or creating help improve fine motor skills and hand-eye coordination.

5. Sense of achievement:

- **Goal Achievement:** Achieving goals linked to hobbies raises one's self-esteem and gives one a sense of achievement.

- **Personal progress:** Acquiring new abilities or becoming proficient in a pastime over time promotes a feeling of competence and personal progress.

6. Stimulation of Creativity:

- **Expression of Self:** Engaging in creative activities enables people to express who they are, which promotes originality and a feeling of self.

- **Innovation and Problem-Solving:** Taking part in creative pursuits fosters the development of creative problem-solving and inventive thinking abilities, which are transferable to other facets of life.

7. Benefits to Mental Health:

- **Coping Mechanism:** Hobbies can be useful coping strategies in trying times, offering a constructive way to let tension and emotions out.

- **Depression Risk Reduction:** Regularly partaking in pleasant activities has been linked to better mental health and a decreased incidence of depression.

8. Time Management and Structure:

- **Healthy Routine:** Hobbies foster a feeling of purpose and order in daily life by helping to create a regimented and satisfying routine.

- **Time Effectively Used:** Hobbies help people manage their time because they offer a meaningful way to spend leisure time.

9. Learning and Adaptability:

- **Continuous Learning:** Learning new things and developing new abilities are common hobbies that encourage a passion for lifetime learning and a curious attitude.

- **Adaptability:** Taking up new interests and becoming accustomed to them might help increase cognitive flexibility and the capacity to accept change.

10. Improved Life Quality:

- **Happy Existence:** Overall, having hobbies makes life happier and more meaningful, which improves people's quality of life in general.

11. Reflective and Spiritual Advantages:

- **Courtesy of Mindfulness:** Creative endeavors, like writing, painting, or meditation, can encourage introspection and mindfulness, which can result in a greater feeling of spirituality and self-awareness.

Brain-Boosting Games and Activities

To enhance brain function and promote cognitive health, incorporating brain-boosting games and activities into your routine can be beneficial.

Here are several ways to support and maximize the effectiveness of these activities:

1. Diverse Cognitive Exercises:

- **Diversity is Crucial:** Take part in a range of brain-boosting activities that focus on various cognitive processes. Add games that test your ability to pay attention, solve problems, remember things, and use logic.

2. Consistent Practice:

- **Regular Engagement:** Include regular brain-boosting activities in your daily routine. Getting long-term cognitive advantages requires consistent practice.

3. Gradual Complexity:

- **Progressive Challenges:** As you gain experience, progressively increase the intricacy of the tasks. This keeps your mind active and keeps you from getting bored.

4. Social Interaction:

- **Multiplayer Games:** Choose socially interactive games that improve cognitive function. Playing card games, board games, or multiplayer internet games is a great way to engage people socially and mentally.

5. Learning New Skills:

- **Continuous Learning:** Take part in activities that call for learning new abilities. The brain's capacity for adaptation and change, known as neuroplasticity, is enhanced and stimulated by learning.

6. Activities for the Cardiovascular System:

- **Physical Exercise:** Regular physical activity—especially aerobic activity—has been associated with enhanced cognitive performance. Play games that sharpen the mind in addition to physical exercises like swimming, dancing, or walking.

7. Well-Rounded Diet:

- **Nutrition for Brain Health:** Maintain cognitive health with a nutrient-rich, well-balanced diet. Vitamins, antioxidants, and omega-3 fatty acids are necessary for proper brain function.

8. Sufficient Sleep:

- **Excellent Rest:** Make sure you get enough good sleep. For memory consolidation and general cognitive function, sleep is essential.

9. Practices of Mindfulness:

- **Mindful Meditation:** Include mindfulness exercises in your daily routine. Relaxation methods and mindful meditation can improve focus and lower stress, which will improve cognitive performance.

10. Maintain Social Interactions:

- **Build Social Networks:** Keep up social relationships and have regular chats. Healthy cognitive function is influenced by meaningful social interactions.

11. Take a risk and push yourself:

- **Go Outside Your Comfort Zone:** Never back down from a difficult endeavor. Tough tasks foster cognitive development, such as mastering an instrument, learning a new language, or completing intricate riddles.

12. Technology Inclusion:

- **Apps for Brain Training:** Examine apps for brain training that include a variety of cognitive activities. Personalized challenges are frequently offered by these apps in response to your performance.

13. Mind-Body Coordination:

- **Coordination Activities:** Take part in mind-body coordination exercises like tai chi, yoga, or dancing. Different cognitive functions are stimulated by these activities.

14. Education and Reading:

- **Ongoing Reading:** Regular reading will keep your mind active. Select a range of subjects and genres to expose your mind to a diversity of information sources.

15. Control Stress:

- **Handle stress effectively:** Use stress-reduction strategies to control your stress levels, such as deep breathing. Cognitive function may be adversely affected by ongoing stress.

16. Enjoyable Activities:

- **Fun and enjoyment:** Select cognitively stimulating pursuits that you truly enjoy. Encouraging mental challenges while having fun increases motivation and engagement.

CHAPTER 6

COPING WITH LOSS AND CHANGE

Navigating Grief and Loss in the Senior Years

Senior year sadness and loss may be a deep and difficult journey to navigate. People may experience the loss of spouses, friends, relatives, or even their own health as they get older. Understanding and addressing the psychological, bodily, and spiritual facets of the mourning process are essential to coping with bereavement. The following are some things to think about and methods for dealing with loss and sadness in your senior years:

1. Validate and Acknowledge Emotions:

- **Allow Feelings:** It's critical that elders recognize and accept their feelings. There are many different ways that grief can appear, such as sadness, anger, guilt, or even relief. Promote honest emotional expression.

2. Ask for Help:

- **Build Social Networks:** Urge elderly people to rely on their social networks—friends, family, and the community—for support. Talking to others and looking for emotional support can be beneficial.

3. Take Part in Support Groups for Bereavement:

- **Community Connection:** Getting involved in grief support groups can help one feel understood and part of a community. Talking about your experiences with other bereaved people can be reassuring and validating.

4. Empathy for Oneself:

- **Treat Yourself with Love:** Remind elderly people to be kind to themselves. There is no "right" way to grieve; it is a personal and distinct process. Promote self-respect and comprehension.

5. Remembrance and Memorialization:

- **Establish Rituals:** Urge elderly people to start customs or take part in memorial events that pay tribute to their departed loved ones. This can be done by doing things like making a memory book, planting a tree, or attending memorial ceremonies.

6. Maintain routines:

Consistency: It can help to feel stable and normal to keep up regular habits while adjusting to life without a loved one.

7. Physical Well-Being:

- **Wellness and Exercise:** Motivate seniors to give their physical well-being first priority. A healthy diet, regular exercise, and enough sleep all support general wellbeing and have a beneficial effect on mood.

8. Spiritual Support: Spiritual Practices Religious or spiritual activities can provide people who believe in spirituality with comfort and a sense of being connected to something greater.

9. Reminiscence Therapy:

- **Consider Good Recollections:** In reminiscence therapy, happy memories are reflected upon. Urge elderly people to recall happy times spent with their loved ones and to tell stories about them.

10. Promote Interests and Hobbies:

- **Involvement in Interests:** Seniors should be encouraged to engage in interests and pastimes they enjoy. Taking up hobbies or creative endeavors can be a healthy way to release feelings.

11. Address Practical Concerns:

- **Financial and Legal Planning:** Help seniors take care of practical issues, such as money and legal issues, pertaining to the loss. By offering assistance in these areas, extra stress can be reduced.

12. Appreciate Life:

- **Pay Attention to the Positive Aspects:** Seniors should be encouraged to celebrate the lives and positive contributions of their loved ones while acknowledging the sadness of loss.

13. Encourage Journaling and Expressive Writing:

Encourage journaling as a means of expressing ideas and feelings. One therapeutic way to handle loss is through writing.

14. Exercise: "Patience and Compassion"; "Non-Judgmental Assistance Provide empathetic and accommodating assistance. Everybody's experience of grief is individual and constitutes a unique journey. Refrain from imposing notions about how someone "should" grieve.

Adapting to Life Transitions and Changes

It can be difficult for seniors to adjust to life transitions and changes, such as retirement, changes in health, the death of a loved one, or changes in housing arrangements. Seniors can use the following tactics to help them deal with and adjust to life transitions:

1. Gratitude and Perception:

- **Recognize Feelings:** When changes in your life occur, give yourself permission to experience and recognize the whole spectrum of emotions. Recognize that life is full of change, and embrace it.

2. Retain a Positive Attitude:

- **Pay Attention to the Positives:** See the good things about the change. This can be an opportunity for personal development, the chance to pursue new interests, or newly discovered spare time.

3. Create a Support System:

Rely on your loved ones. Consult your family, friends, or a support group for assistance. To build a sense of connection, express your emotions and worries to people you can trust.

4. Establish Reasonable Expectations:

- **Reasonable Prognosis:** During the shift, give yourself reasonable expectations. Recognize that change takes time, and it's acceptable to proceed cautiously at first.

5. Create New Routines:

- **Create Routines:** Establish new routines that correspond with your life's changes. A daily routine that is well organized can provide one with a feeling of security and control.

6. Remain Intense and Vigorous:

- **Exercise and Mental Focus:** Take part in mental and physical activities to stay well. A sense of purpose is enhanced by social interactions, hobbies, and exercise.

7. Survive Lifelong Learning:

- **Educational Possibilities:** Accept chances for lifelong learning. This could entail learning new skills, attending classes, or picking up a new pastime.

8. Plan for the Future:

- **Future Considerations:** Make future plans by taking your desires and inclinations into account. To provide a sense of security, this may entail making plans for your finances, legal situation, or medical care.

9. Put an emphasis on self-care:

- **Put your wellbeing first:** Make self-care a priority to keep your body and mind healthy. This entails getting enough sleep, eating healthy food, and engaging in enjoyable activities.

10. Discover New Interests:

- **Inquisitiveness and Research:** Develop your curiosity by taking up new hobbies and pursuits. Personal development and a sense of fulfillment may result from this.

11. Express Yourself Creatively:

- **Creative outlets:** During periods of transition, express your thoughts and feelings through creative mediums like writing, painting, or music.

12. Volunteer and Give Back:

- **Community Involvement:** Take part in volunteer work to support your neighborhood. Giving to others can give one a feeling of connection and purpose.

13. Maintain Communication:

- **Social Exchanges:** Keep up your social relationships with your family and friends. Social interaction and regular communication are beneficial to emotional health.

14. Build Resilience:

- **Cultivate Resilience:** Resilience can be developed by seeing obstacles as chances for improvement. Take lessons from past mistakes and keep an open mind when facing new situations.

15. Celebrate Successes:

- **Recognize Advancements:** Recognize little victories along the way. Acknowledge your growth and tenacity as you adjust to new circumstances.

16. Relaxation and Mindfulness:

- **Mind-Body Techniques:** To reduce stress and preserve inner peace, engage in mindfulness, meditation, or relaxation exercises.

17. Remain Knowledgeable:

- **Well-Informed Choice-Making:** Remain aware of the changes you are going through. Having knowledge lessens uncertainty and gives you the ability to make wise judgments.

Finding Purpose and Meaning in Later Life

Finding purpose and meaning in later life is a deeply personal and fulfilling journey. As individuals age, there may be changes in roles, routines, and relationships, prompting a search for renewed purpose and fulfillment. Here are some strategies to help discover and cultivate purpose and meaning in later life:

1. Reflect on Core Values:

Spend some time thinking about your fundamental ideas and principles. Think about your priorities and the things that bring significance to your life. Knowing your values lays the groundwork for leading a purposeful life.

2. Set Meaningful Goals:

Establish clear, purposeful objectives that are consistent with your principles. These objectives may have to do with developing oneself, fostering relationships, helping others, or trying new things.

3. Explore Interests and Passions:

Rekindle old passions or discover brand-new ones. Taking part in activities you love, whether they be hobbies, artistic endeavors, or learning a new skill, gives your life meaning and happiness.

4. Embrace Lifelong Learning:

Foster an attitude of perpetual learning. Participate in workshops, enroll in classes, or study new topics on your own. Acquiring knowledge not only piques the intellect but also helps foster a feeling of direction.

5. Volunteer and Contribute:

Look for chances to give back to your community or volunteer. By improving the lives of others and creating a link to a greater cause, volunteering gives one a sense of purpose.

6. Cultivate Meaningful Relationships:

Foster and maintain meaningful connections. A feeling of purpose and belonging is enhanced by socializing with friends, family, and neighbors.

7. Share Wisdom and Experience:

Talk to people about your knowledge, insight, and experiences from life. There are several ways to leave a lasting legacy and find purpose in your work, including teaching, mentoring, and even writing about your experiences.

8. Connect with Nature:

Take time to enjoy the outdoors, whether it's through gardening, strolling, or just being in nature. Having a connection to nature can give one a sense of purpose and calm.

9. Practice gratitude:

Develop thankfulness by thinking back on the things in your life that are good. Positive thinking and a sense of purpose are fostered by journaling your thankfulness or by expressing your gratitude on a regular basis.

10. Take Part in Spiritual Practices: Experiment with or hone your spiritual disciplines. This could be engaging in contemplative practices that are consistent with your beliefs, such as meditation or religious activities.

11. Establish Reasonable Expectations:

Make reasonable expectations for yourself. Recognize that discovering your mission is a process that takes time to perfect. Accept the path and practice self-compassion.

12. Create a Daily Routine:

Make time each day for meaningful activities that you find to be important. A regimented schedule gives your day direction and organization.

13. Celebrating Achievements:

No matter how tiny, take pride in and acknowledge your accomplishments. Acknowledging your contributions and successes strengthens your sense of purpose and raises your self-esteem.

14. Acknowledge and Adjust to Changing Roles:

Recognize and adjust to shifting roles and duties. Accept the chances that come with transitioning into new phases of life and discover significance in the changing facets of who you are.

15. Remain physically active:

Make exercise a priority, even if it's only light duty. Frequent movement enhances general wellbeing and has a great effect on your sense of mission.

16. Appreciate Creativity:

Take part in artistic, literary, musical, or other forms of expression. Self-fulfillment and self-discovery have an outlet in creativity.

CHAPTER 7

CREATING A HEALTHY ENVIRONMENT

The Impact of Physical Environment on Mental Well-being

Mental health can be significantly impacted by one's physical surroundings. People's moods, stress levels, and general mental health can be influenced by the places where they live, work, and spend their time. The following are some significant ways that the physical surroundings might affect mental health:

1. Sunlight and Natural Light:

- **Good Impact:** Natural light exposure has been linked to better sleep, higher energy levels, and happier moods. Serotonin is a neurotransmitter that helps with feelings of wellbeing and is stimulated by sunlight.

2. Nature and Green Spaces:

- **Reduction of Stress:** Stress reduction has been associated with access to parks, green areas, and natural settings. Time spent in nature enhances mood, encourages relaxation, and benefits mental health in general.

3. Noise Levels:

- **Effect on Tension:** Excessive noise, particularly loud or continuous noise, can exacerbate anxiety and stress. The mind can be calmed by being in a quiet or serene setting.

4. Clean and Tidy Spaces:

- **Clutter and Mental Clarity:** Mental clarity and emotions of overwhelm can both be positively impacted by a neat and orderly workspace. Disorganized areas can increase stress and make it difficult to concentrate.

5. Aesthetics and Color:

- **Mood-Releasing Effect:** Mood can be affected by aesthetics and color. While cool colors can produce a quiet and calm atmosphere, bright and warm colors can arouse sensations of vitality and happiness.

6. Temperature and Ventilation:

- **Satisfaction and Efficiency:** Physical comfort is influenced by appropriate ventilation and temperature, which in turn impacts mental health.

Intense heat or inadequate airflow can cause pain and reduce efficiency.

7. Space Personalization:

- **Ownership Feeling:** Customizing one's home or work environment can foster a feeling of identity and ownership. Having a sense of belonging to one's surroundings is beneficial to mental health.

8. Security and Safety:

- **Quality of Mind:** Peace of mind is fostered by an atmosphere that is viewed as safe and secure. A feeling of safety can help people feel less stressed and anxious, which is important for mental health.

9. Mobility and Accessibility:

- **Independence and Self-Governance:** Particularly for older adults, easily navigable and mobile spaces enhance a person's feeling of freedom and autonomy. This may have a favorable mental well-being impact.

10. Social Spaces and Connection:

- **Community Engagement:** Areas that promote social contact and connections with people help people feel like they belong and build a sense of community, which improves mental health.

11. Workplace:

- **Life Balance Between Work and Life:** The mental health of employees can be positively impacted by a work environment that promotes work-life balance, fosters teamwork, and offers chances for breaks.

12. Technology Utilization:

- **Technology Equilibrated:** Technology integration may have an effect on mental health. Even though technology fosters human connection, prolonged screen time or continuous use can exacerbate stress. Technology use must be balanced.

13. Cultural Sensitivity:

- **Inclusive Environments:** People from a variety of backgrounds feel more at home and content in environments that are inclusive and attentive to cultural differences.

14. Transitional Areas:

- **Changes and Transitions:** Environments that ease transitions can be beneficial to mental health, particularly during significant life changes. This comprises areas that offer solace during transitional times.

Simplifying and Organizing: Decluttering for Mental Health

Decluttering is a common way to simplify and organize, which can have a significant positive impact on mental health. An environment that is messy and unorganized can aggravate stress, overwhelm, and a sensation of mental heaviness. However, keeping a room tidy, orderly, and uncomplicated can help with focus, mental clarity, and calmness.

Decluttering can have the following beneficial effects on mental health:

1. Minimization of Visual Diversion:

- **Spatiotemporal Focus and Concentration:** Less visual distractions mean that it is easier to focus and concentrate in a clutter-free environment. This can lessen mental exhaustion and increase productivity.

2. Promotion of Calm and Serenity:

- **Reduction of Stress:** Calm is enhanced by an environment that is ordered and uncomplicated. Decluttering itself has the potential to be therapeutic, lowering stress and fostering a calmer home or office environment.

3. Enhanced Output:

- **Reduction in Consumption:** Time and resources can be used more effectively in an organized space. Things are easy to find, and unneeded clutter doesn't get in the way of doing chores.

4. Improved Decision-Making:

- **Clear Thinking:** Clear thinking is encouraged in an environment devoid of clutter. Decision fatigue is decreased when decisions are made more simply, such as selecting what to eat or wear.

5. Sentiment of Achievement:

- **Advantageous Feedback:** Upon finishing the decluttering process, one feels in control and accomplished. Self-worth and confidence can rise as a result of this encouraging feedback.

6. Improved Sleep Quality:

- **Calm Ambience:** A bedroom devoid of clutter fosters a calm ambience that enhances the quality of sleep. A calm sleeping environment is beneficial to mental wellness in general.

7. Enhanced Movement and Flow:

- **Easier Navigation:** Cleared space makes things easier to move around and flow through. This is especially crucial in regions where mobility is necessary for overall health.

8. Optimized Living Spaces:

- **Functional Design:** Living areas that are purposefully and functionally organized make for a more comfortable and happy living environment. This may have a good effect on happiness and mood in general.

9. Decrease in Stress:

- **Social Release:** By lessening the overwhelming sensation that comes with being in a disorderly or chaotic environment, decluttering can offer emotional relief. A neat environment fosters control.

10. Favorable Effect on Bonds:

- **Common Areas:** Decluttering helps promote peace and healthy relationships in shared living areas. Everyone tends to enjoy an environment that is more orderly and clean.

11. Encouragement of Mindfulness:

- **Present Moment Awareness:** Decluttering promotes mindfulness, which is the act of choosing what to keep and discard with intention and being present in the moment.

12. Financial Consciousness:

- **Awareness of Possessions:** Organizing things makes one more conscious of their holdings and may deter wasteful purchasing. This financial awareness might have a good effect on one's general wellbeing.

13. Developing Positive Habits:

- **Upkeep:** After a space is cleared out, keeping it organized becomes a healthy habit. A sense of stability and order is facilitated by consistent routines.

14. Emotional Detox:

- **Leaving Behind:** Letting go of things that are no longer useful is a common step in the decluttering process. This emotional and mental space-freeing process of releasing can be immensely relieving.

15. **Self-Care Promotion:

- **Putting Well-Being First:** Clearing out clutter is a type of self-care. Making your living area a priority shows that you care about your health and well-being.

Nature Therapy: Connecting with the Outdoors

Spending time in natural settings is a key component of connecting with nature, also known as ecotherapy or nature therapy, which aims to enhance mental and emotional health. This type of natural treatment highlights the therapeutic qualities of natural environments while acknowledging the beneficial effects of nature on mental health. The following are some ways that spending time in nature can serve as a kind of natural therapy:

1. Forest bathing (Shinrin-Yoku):

- **Nature immersion:** A Japanese custom called "forest bathing" entails submerging oneself in a woodland setting. This calm, contemplative practice promotes sensory investigation and has been linked to lowered stress levels, happier moods, and increased general wellbeing.

2. Nature Walks and Hiking:

- **Activities in the Natural World:** Walking or hiking in natural environments offers the advantages of both physical activity and exposure to the outdoors. It can improve mood, lessen anxiety, and improve thinking.

3. Outdoor Meals and Picnics:

- **Social Interaction in Nature:** In a natural environment, dining al fresco with loved ones promotes social cohesion. Positive relationships and a feeling of community may benefit from this.

4. Gardening:

- **Interaction with Hands:** Working with the soil and plants firsthand is part of gardening. Engaging in this activity has been associated with feelings of accomplishment, less stress, and an improved mood.

5. Mindfulness and Outdoor Meditation:

- **Mindful Presence:** People can establish a sense of peace and presence in the outdoors while connecting with nature by engaging in mindfulness or meditation practices.

6. Beach Therapy:

- **Atlantic Conditions:** Time spent at the beach has been linked to stress relief and relaxation. The feeling of sand beneath your feet, the sound of breaking waves, and the seaside scenery can all be soothing.

7. Artistic Expression:

- **Nature Journaling:** Observations, feelings, and thoughts regarding the natural world are all documented in a nature notebook. It offers a chance for introspection and artistic expression.

8. Stargazing:

- **Establishing a Connection with the Universe:** One can have a meditative and inspirational experience while stargazing. Stargazing promotes introspection and a feeling of interconnectedness with the cosmos.

9. Outdoor Yoga:

- **Mind-Body Connection:** The benefits of physical exertion, mindfulness, and connecting with nature are combined when practicing yoga outside. It builds a bond with the natural world and encourages flexibility and relaxation.

10. Retreats in Nature:

- **Deep Nature Experiences:** Natural retreat locations offer an immersive experience that enables people to detach from everyday stressors and re-establish a long-term connection with the natural world.

11. Wilderness Therapy:

- **Therapeutic Outdoor Programs:** Therapeutic interventions take place in natural environments as part of wilderness therapy. Through outdoor experiences, it aims to foster personal development, self-discovery, and healing.

12. Birdwatching:

- **Observation and Reflection:** Observation and introspection are encouraged by birdwatching. It connects people with the variety of bird life around them and offers a peaceful, reflective experience.

13. Water Features Found in Nature:

- **Lakes, Rivers, and Waterfalls:** There is a relaxing impact when one is near natural water features. Relaxation is enhanced by the sound of flowing water and the attractiveness of aquatic settings.

14. Creativity and Outdoor Art:

- **Artistic Expression:** Painting, drawing, or sculpting outside fosters artistic creativity that is influenced by the natural world.

15. Nature Soundscapes:

- **Taking in the Sounds of Nature:** It can be calming and relaxing to listen to the sounds of nature, such as birdsong, rustling leaves, or flowing water.

CHAPTER 8

FINANCIAL WELLNESS FOR SENIORS

Financial Stress and its Effect on Mental Health

The strain and anxiety people feel as a result of their financial circumstances is referred to as financial stress. It can be caused by a number of things, such as debt, unemployment, low income, unforeseen costs, or worries about the future. Stress related to money can have a significant negative impact on mental health, affecting both general mental health and emotional well-being. The following are some ways that stress related to money can impact mental health:

1. Trouble and Anxiety:

- **Ongoing Concern:** Anxiety and worry about money-related matters are frequently brought on by financial hardship. People could feel scared and uneasy about their financial situation in the future.

2. Depression:

- **Hopelessness Feelings:** Extended financial strain might exacerbate depressive symptoms by adding to powerlessness and hopelessness. An ongoing sense of hopelessness and depression may result from the strain to fulfill financial obligations.

3. Disturbances in Sleep and Insomnia:

- **Affect on Sleep:** Stress related to money might interfere with sleep cycles, resulting in insomnia or other sleep disorders. Prolonged financial concerns can make it difficult to get to sleep or stay asleep.

4. Physical Health Issues:

- **Illnesses Associated with Stress:** An increased risk of stress-related health problems, such as headaches, digestive troubles, and cardiovascular disorders, is associated with long-term financial stress. Because of the mind-body link, physical symptoms of mental stress can also occur.

5. Impact on Relationships:

- **Difficulty with Personal Connections:** Relationships with friends, partners, and family can be strained by financial stress. Money-related disputes can occur, which heightens stress and strains relationships.

6. Decreased Productivity and Concentration:

- **Workplace Challenges:** Stress related to money can have a negative impact on focus, output, and job performance at work. Focusing on work can be difficult for some people because of their financial worries.

7. Shame and Guilt Feelings:

- **Impact on Self-Esteem:** Feelings of shame and guilt can arise from financial challenges, especially if people believe that their financial circumstances are a reflection of their own shortcomings. Self-esteem may be badly impacted by this.

8. Avoidance Behavior:

- **Steer clear of financial matters:** Certain people may exhibit avoidance tendencies in relation to money matters. This may increase general tension and result in a lack of proactive financial management.

9. Affect on Making Decisions:

- **Reduced Cognitive Ability:** Stress related to money can impede cognitive function, which impacts one's capacity to make decisions. Those who are struggling financially may find it difficult to make wise decisions.

10. Withdrawal and Isolation:

- **Social Disengagement:** Social disengagement might result from financial stress because people may avoid social situations because they are worried about their bills. This seclusion might worsen mental health issues and lead to feelings of loneliness.

11. Risk of Substance Abuse Increased:

- **Reduction Strategies:** Some people may use drugs or alcohol to help them deal with the stress and anxiety that come with having money problems. Substance abuse problems may arise from this.

12. Suicidal Thoughts:

- **Severe Situations:** Prolonged financial stress can trigger suicidal thoughts in extreme situations, particularly when paired with other circumstances. Seeking support and assistance is crucial if you're having these kinds of ideas.

Planning for Retirement: Tips for Financial Security

A happy life in your later years and financial security are ensured by making retirement plans. As you make retirement plans, keep the following important principles and advice in mind:

1. Get Started Early:

- **Compounding Power:** The longer your money has to compound, the earlier you should start saving for retirement. To get the most out of retirement funds, start making contributions as soon as you can.

2. Create Specific Objectives Describe your lifestyle and spending. Estimate your future spending and decide on your retirement lifestyle. Take into account things like travel, healthcare, and recreational activities. A clear set of objectives will enable you to determine the required amount of savings.

3. Create a Comprehensive Budget:

- **Understand Current Spending:** Examine your out-of-pocket costs and make a detailed budget. Find areas where you can save more money so that you have more for retirement.

4. Develop Your Retirement Accounts:

- **Make IRA and 401(k) contributions:** Utilize retirement plans offered by your work, such as 401(k)s, and make enough contributions to qualify for any corporate matching. Consider making contributions to individual retirement accounts (IRAs) as well.

5. Diversify Investments:

- **Asset Allocation:** To reduce risk, diversify the investments in your portfolio. Depending on your time horizon and risk tolerance, think about a combination of stocks, bonds, and other investments.

6. Emergency Fund:

- **Financial Safety Net:** Keep an emergency reserve on hand to pay for unforeseen costs. Having a safety net lessens the likelihood that unanticipated events will force one to withdraw from retirement funds.

7. Healthcare Planning:

- **Recognize Medicare and Add-on Insurance:** Learn about your Medicare alternatives, and if there are any gaps in your coverage, think about getting additional insurance. Include healthcare costs in your retirement savings plan.

8. Take Into Account Long-Term Care Insurance:

- **Protection Against Healthcare Costs:** Long-term care insurance can assist in shielding your assets from the hefty expenses of continued medical care that may arise in the future.

9. Management of Debt:

- **Remove Debt with a High Interest Rate:** Prioritize debt repayment with a high interest rate before you retire. Financial stress in retirement can be considerably decreased by being debt-free.

10. Optimization of Social Security:

- **Recognize Your Social Security Options:** Learn about the guidelines and available alternatives for receiving Social Security payments. Higher monthly payments may be the consequence of delaying the start of benefits.

11. Continued Learning and Skill Building:

- **Remain Marketable:** To remain employable in the event that you decide to take up part-time employment after retirement, think about learning new skills or going back to school. Having more money can be advantageous.

12. Develop a Plan for Withdrawal:

- **Achievable Withdrawal Rate:** Create a plan for taking money out of retirement accounts. A popular recommendation is the "4% rule," which states that you should take out 4% of your retirement funds each year to help maintain sustainability.

13. Examine and modify:

- **Evaluate Your Plan Frequently:** Review your retirement plan on a regular basis and make any necessary revisions. Adjustments to your approach can be necessary if your spending, way of life, or the state of the market change.

14. Estate Planning:

- **Make a Will and Name Trustees:** Make arrangements for how your assets will be distributed by naming beneficiaries on retirement accounts and drafting a will.

15. Stay Informed:

- **Be Aware of Changes:** Keep up with changes to the financial markets, retirement laws, and tax laws. Knowing about these modifications enables you to modify your plan appropriately.

16. Retain a Healthy Lifestyle:

- **Give Physical and Mental Health First Priority** An active and satisfying retirement can be facilitated by leading a healthy lifestyle. Make healthy eating, regular exercise, and mental health-promoting activities your top priorities.

CHAPTER 9

MAINTAINING A POSITIVE OUTLOOK

The Power of Positive Thinking in Aging

The ability to think positively can have a significant impact on aging, impacting both mental and physical health. As people get older, keeping a positive outlook can help them live better lives, have better health outcomes, and be more resilient when faced with obstacles. Among the many benefits of positive thinking as we age are the following:

1. More Mental Well-Being:

- **Decreased Stress and Anxiety: There** is a correlation between positive thinking and reduced stress and anxiety. Seniors who have a positive mindset are better able to handle life's obstacles and maintain greater mental health.

2. Optimism and Resilience:

- **Adaptation to Change: Thinking** positively encourages optimism and resilience, which helps people adjust to life's ups and downs and unexpected situations more skillfully.

3. Cognitive Benefits:

- **Enhanced Cognitive Performance:** Research points to a possible connection between improved cognitive performance in older adults and an optimistic outlook. By lowering the chance of cognitive deterioration and preserving cognitive capacities, positive thinking may help.

4. Benefits to Physical Health:

- **Reduced Risk of Chronic Illnesses:** There is a correlation between positive thinking and a decreased risk of chronic illnesses. Positive outlooks on life have been linked to improved general health and a lower risk of various health disorders in seniors.

5. Longevity:

- **Improved Lifespan:** Research indicates that preserving an optimistic outlook could potentially lead to a longer lifespan. Positive thinkers frequently lead healthier lifestyles, make wiser judgments regarding their health, and participate in activities that advance wellbeing.

6. Stronger Social Connections:

- **Improved Social Communication:** optimistic social interactions are frequently attracted to optimistic folks. Keeping an optimistic attitude helps strengthen social ties, lessen feelings of loneliness, and increase a sense of belonging.

7. Relationship Quality:

- **Favourable Impact on Relationships:** Relationships with family and friends are healthier when positive thinking is present. It encourages candid dialogue, encouragement from one another, and a spirit of optimism among everyone.

8. Emotional Wellness:

- **Enhanced Contentment:** Positive thinking is strongly associated with higher levels of satisfaction and happiness. Maintaining an optimistic perspective on life can help you age with greater joy and fulfillment.

9. Mind-Body Connection:

- **Encouraging Well-Being:** The mind-body link links positive thinking to increased immune system performance and decreased inflammation as ways to impact physical health.

10. Meaning and Purpose:

- **Increased Feeling of Purpose:** Keeping an optimistic outlook on life might help one feel more meaningful and purposeful in it. Having a sense of purpose is linked to better mental and emotional health.

11. Adaptive Coping Techniques:

- **Successful Coping with Difficulties:** Challenges are typically approached by positive thinkers with a problem-solving mentality. Seniors who use this adaptive coping approach can overcome obstacles and come up with useful solutions.

12. Engagement in Lifelong Learning:

- **Inquiry and Development:** Positivity fosters inquisitiveness and a passion for lifelong learning. Positive-thinking seniors might be more likely to pursue personal development, take up new hobbies, and discover new interests.

13. Gratitude Exercises:

- **Attention to Gratitude:** Gratitude practice is one facet of positive thinking. Seniors who practice thankfulness may find that they are more appreciative of the good things in their lives and that their level of life satisfaction increases.

14. An Active Lifestyle:

- **Incentives for Exercise:** Those who think positively are frequently more inclined to exercise. Frequent exercise promotes both physical and mental well-being, which is an essential component of healthy aging.

15. Awareness of the Present Moment and Mindfulness:

- **Mindful Aging:** Concentrating on the here and now and practicing mindfulness are frequently linked to positive thinking. Growing older can be made more enjoyable overall with mindful aging.

Gratitude Practices for Mental Wellness

Gratitude exercises are an effective way to support mental health. Focusing on and valuing the good things in life is a deliberate way to cultivate thankfulness. The following list of thankfulness exercises might support mental health:

1. Writing a Journal of Gratitude:

- **Daily Thought:** Keep a gratitude notebook in which you list three things every day for which you are grateful. Recalling happy moments helps refocus your attention on the positive aspects of your life.

2.Thank You Notes:

- **Sending Words of Appreciation:** Thank the person who has made a good difference in your life with a letter. For a stronger connection, think about delivering the letter in person.

3. Mindful Gratitude"

- **Awareness of the Present:** By paying attention to the here and now and expressing your gratitude for what you have right now, you may practice mindfulness. This may be done during regular activities or while meditating.

4. Appreciation Jar:

- **Spatial Reminder:** Make a thankfulness jar into which you will periodically add notes of thanksgiving for good deeds, accomplishments, or moments. To encourage good sentiments, go over the notes from time to time.

5. Affirmations of Gratitude:

- **Positive Self-Talk:** Make it a daily habit to say affirmations of thankfulness. Confirm the good things in your life and show gratitude for your connections, abilities, and chances.

6. Gratitude Walks:

- **Walking with Mind:** Go for a stroll with the purpose of concentrating on thankfulness. Take in the beauty all around you, enjoy the feelings of nature, and think back on the good things in your life.

7. Rituals of Gratitude:

- **Daily or Evening Routine:** Allocate particular periods of time each day for contemplating thankfulness. This might be something you do every morning or as a nightly ritual.

8. Thank You Partner:

- **Give to a Friend:** Share daily or weekly observations on appreciation with a friend or family member. Talking about your experiences with others might increase their beneficial effects.

9. Meditation of Gratitude:

- **Guided Meditation:** To concentrate your thoughts on appreciation and thankfulness, try using guided gratitude meditation sessions. Numerous meditation applications include gratitude-focused sessions.

10. Gratitude Calendar:

- **Spatial Monitoring:** Make a thankfulness calendar in which you write a word or symbol for each day that you are thankful for. This graphic depiction might act as a memory of happy times past.

11. Mealtime Appreciation:

- **Thank You:** Before meals, take a minute to be grateful for the food, the company you're with, and other blessings in your life.

12. Appreciation amid Difficulties:

- **Discovering Positive Aspects:** When faced with obstacles, look for the good things that happened or the lessons you learned. This change in viewpoint can foster thankfulness and perseverance under trying circumstances.

13. Acts of Generosity:

- **Returning the Favor:** Participate in impromptu acts of kindness, and give to show your thanks. This might be giving back to the community, volunteering, or carrying out tiny acts of kindness.

14. Technology Detox:

- **Removing the Plug:** Take a vacation from technology and enjoy how basic life is. Removing your screen time enables you to become more aware of your local environment and more in the moment.

15. Community Support:

- **Gratitude Group:** Join or start a gratitude group where people can express their thanks to one another. The benefits of practicing thankfulness may be amplified by this support from the community.

16. Reflecting on Achievements:

- **Acknowledging Accomplishments:**

Contemplate your accomplishments and offer thanks for the abilities and efforts that made them possible.

17. Gratitude Challenges:

- **Goals-Setting:** Take part in thankfulness challenges, where the goal is to identify and express gratitude for a certain number of items per day.

Embracing Aging with a Positive Mindset

Adopting a viewpoint that emphasizes the possibilities, experiences, and knowledge that come with getting older is essential to embracing aging with a positive outlook. The following techniques can assist you in developing an optimistic outlook as you get older:

1. Develop Self-Compassion:

- **Accept Your Imperfections:** Be nice and understanding to yourself. Recognize that growing older is a normal process and that imperfection is acceptable.

2. Stay in the Now:

- **Mindful Living:** Remain in the present moment by engaging in mindfulness exercises. Instead of thinking about the past or worrying about the future, take time to enjoy the experiences and relationships you have in your life at this moment.

3. Celebrate Achievements:

- **Consider Your Achievements:** Give your life's accomplishments and significant anniversaries some thought and commemorate them. This kind of introspection may help one feel proud and accomplished.

4. Appreciate Lifelong Learning:

- **Inquisitiveness and Development:** Keep an inquisitive and receptive mentality. Accept the chance to learn and develop yourself, whether it's by taking up new hobbies, gaining new skills, or pursuing academic interests.

5. Maintain Social Media Presence:

- **Build Connections:** Take care of your social networks. Maintain relationships with your community, family, and friends. Having meaningful relationships enhances one's wellbeing and sense of purpose.

6. Adopt a health-conscious lifestyle: Put your wellbeing first. Prioritize maintaining a healthy lifestyle with frequent exercise, a well-balanced diet, and enough sleep. Mental and physical health are positively correlated.

7. Positive Self-Talk:

- **Uplift Yourself:** Engage in constructive self-talk. Affirmations that reaffirm your talents and qualities might help you counter negative thinking.

8. Participate in Meaningful Activities:

- **Discover Meaning:** Take part in things that make you happy and give you a sense of direction. This may include taking up a hobby, volunteering, or making donations to organizations that are important to you.

9. Acclimate to Change:

- **Adaptable Mentality:** Have an adaptable attitude and welcome change. See obstacles as chances for development and adaptability. Positivity is enhanced by resilience in the face of change.

10. Retain a Sense of Humor:

- **Find Laughter:** Develop a sense of humor and discover happiness in the little things in life. Laughter can be a very useful tool for keeping a good outlook and has several health advantages.

11. Express Gratitude:

- **Take Stock of Your Blessings:** By consistently recognizing and appreciating the good things in your life, you may cultivate thankfulness. This may help foster a more upbeat outlook.

12. Establish New Objectives:

- **Make sensible goals:** Set new objectives that reflect your beliefs and areas of interest. Setting meaningful objectives might help you stay motivated and on course.

13. Accept Aged Wisdom:

- **Consider Wisdom:** Accept the knowledge that age provides. Consider the lessons you have learned and the experiences you have had in life. Talk to people about your wisdom.

14. Remain Tech-Aware:

- **Adopt Technology:** Learn about and make use of technology to stay in touch with the world that is changing. It can support your further education, social interaction, and engagement.

15. Express Yourself Creatively:

- **Expression of Art:** Investigate your artistic side in writing, painting, or music. Being creative and expressing yourself may be rewarding experiences.

16. Develop Resilience:

- **Take Lessons from Difficulties:** See obstacles as chances to improve and learn. Resilience building enables you to overcome adversity with courage and hope.

17. Create a Positive Environment for Yourself:

- **Good Influences:** Whether it's via your actual surroundings, your relationships, or the material you watch, surround yourself with good influences.

18. Practice Acceptance:

- **Embrace Change:** Acknowledge that life is full of change on a regular basis. A more tranquil and contented state of mind might result from accepting the changes that occur with becoming older.

19. Celebrate Aging:

- **Appreciate the Journey:** Enjoy the insight that comes with growing older and the journey it takes you on. Realize that every stage of life offers special chances and delights of its own.

CONCLUSION

To sum up, the book "How to Reduce Stress and Improve Your Mental Health for Seniors" provides a comprehensive and useful manual for overcoming the particular difficulties that come with growing older while placing a high priority on mental health. The book intends to enable seniors to embrace a positive mentality, develop resilience, and adopt practical techniques to improve their general mental health through a thorough investigation of many issues.

Understanding the aging brain and the significance of preserving cognitive function is the first step on the path. The goal of the book is to destigmatize mental health problems in the elderly and promote candid discussions about emotional well-being by addressing typical mental health concerns that older adults face. The book "Breaking the Stigma: Addressing Mental Health in the Elderly" highlights the importance of identifying and resolving mental health issues among the elderly.

The book delves into the complexities of stress, defining it and examining how it affects mental health. By using relaxation techniques, readers may uncover the mind-body link, identify stress triggers in seniors, and comprehend the cumulative effects of chronic stress. Seniors who get practical guidance on the benefits of exercise, proper eating, and adequate sleep in reducing stress are better prepared to lead balanced, healthy lives.

The book's main theme is social connectedness, with an emphasis on the detrimental effects of social isolation on senior mental health. It is acknowledged that human interaction plays a crucial role in creating a sense of community and providing emotional support when discussing strategies for establishing and preserving social relationships. Utilizing technology to enhance social connection presents a modern method of being in touch in a constantly changing digital environment.

The book also explores the significance of mental exercises, hobbies, and creative pursuits in keeping the mind sharp, promoting cognitive health, and providing a source of joy and fulfillment. It offers practical guidance on navigating grief, adapting to life transitions, and finding purpose and meaning in later life, acknowledging the diverse challenges and opportunities that come with aging.

The influence of the physical surroundings on mental health is emphasized, stressing the need to clear clutter, spend time in nature, and design environments that support an optimistic outlook. The book also acknowledges the financial strain that seniors may have and offers information on organizations that might help with financial difficulties, encouraging a holistic approach to general well-being.

"How to Reduce Stress and Improve Your Mental Health for Seniors" is essentially a source of information and inspiration for seniors who want to age gracefully, optimistically, and with a proactive attitude toward mental wellness. Through a blend of scientific knowledge, useful advice, and a sensitive comprehension of the distinct circumstances faced by the elderly, the book aims to enable its readers to face aging with dignity, direction, and optimal mental well-being.